GoAndPractice®

Rudimental Vocabulary for the Progressive Drummer

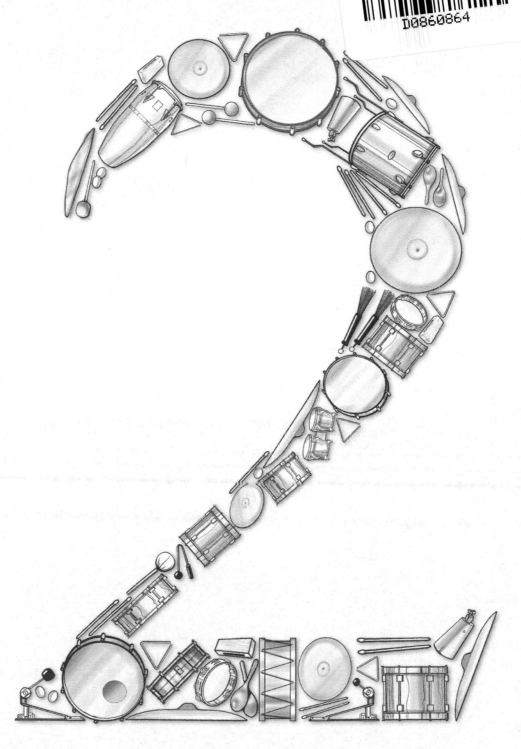

Alec Tackmann

Special thanks to those who have helped in creating this book

Michael King for creating the cover and interior artwork.
Karen Barrie for the design and layout.
Matt Meyer for the photography.
John Sievers for grammatical edits.
Judy Reishus for the presentation guidance.

Also thanks to
My longest-standing and most influential drum teachers Scott Ollhoff,
Rick Considine, and Terri Lyne Carrington.
Mark McKenzie for the years of invaluable career advice.
Berklee College of Music for an excellent four years of learning.
Humes & Berg Mfg. Co., Inc. for the support and top-notch drum cases.

And of course
Thanks to friends and family for the encouragement.
Thank you for choosing this book.

Alec Tackmann

ISBN 978-0-9861950-1-3

©2015

GOANDPRACTICE is the registered trademark of Alec
Tackmann and is used under a license from Alec Tackmann.
GOANDPRACTICE is registered with the United States
Trademark Office, registration number 4831437.

Please address inquiries to:
Alec Tackmann
www.alectackmann.com

$14.95

GoAndPractice® 2

Table of Contents

Forward 7
Technique 8
Double Stroke Roll 10
Inverted Double Stroke Roll 11
Drags 12
Buzz Roll 13
Rooftop Accents 14
Review 15
Single Stroke Roll 16
Three Stroke Ruffs 17
Four Stroke Ruffs 18
Five Stroke Ruffs 19
Paradiddle 20
Paradiddle Variations 21
Review 22
Eighth Note Triplets 23
Eighth Note Triplets/Straight Eighth Notes 24
Sixteenth Note Triplets 25
Quarter Note Triplets/Half Note Triplets 26
Review 27
Seven Stroke Roll 28
Double Paradiddle 29
Paradiddlediddle 30
Six Stroke Roll 31
Review 32
Ratamacue 33
Double Ratamacue/Triple Ratamacue 34
Flam Accent 35
Swiss Triplet 36
Review 37
Flam Paradiddle 38
Flam Tap 39
Flammed Mill 40
Flamacue 41
Pataflafla 42
Flam Drags 43
Swing Eighth Notes 44
Final Review 45
Thirty-Second Notes 46
Rudimental Slash Marks 47
Review 48
Glossary 51

Forward

This book is a study of the most common rudiments and their more advanced reading concepts. In percussion, rudiments are designated combinations of single, double, flam, and buzz strokes that appear so frequently in music they are each given their own name.

Each page is dedicated to one rudiment followed by examples of its variations and structure. In addition to being a reference tool, this book is also written as an exercise guide for each rudiment. Repetition of each passage is important in developing dexterity. Practicing along with a metronome will ensure accurate placement of each stroke.

Alec Tackmann

Technique

Holding the drumsticks with a healthy technique is very important in becoming a good player. Remember, *different techniques can be necessary for different playing situations.* While the rules below will apply for most general purposes, different grips will be used depending on what type of drum you are playing, what style of music you will be performing, or what your specific ensemble requires.

Grip

- Place thumb on the side of the stick.
- The index finger will be slightly in front of the thumb.
- The middle finger will be slightly behind the thumb.
- Wrap the ring and pinky fingers around the base of the stick.
- Approximately one inch of the stick should remain beyond the pinky finger.
- Hold the stick loosely, but keep all fingers on the stick.

Hand Positioning

- In most situations, the back of your hands should remain up.
- Be sure the tips of the sticks hit within approximately two inches of each other for tone consistency.
- Try to hold the sticks at a 90-degree angle.
- Your elbows may either stay relaxed or stick out.

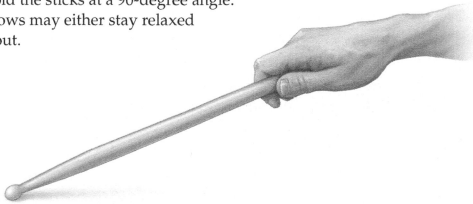

If you are doing all of this correctly, you should be able to see the butt end of the stick over the top of your wrist while the tips of the sticks are down:

The Stroke
The stroke will be generated from a mixture of finger and wrist movement.
Let the stick bounce back after hitting the drum using the stick's natural inertia.
For most situations, be sure to only make one "tap" sound; do not press the stick into the head.

"Do Not's"
Do not put your index finger on the top of the stick.
Do not stick out your pinky fingers, *especially during rolls.*
Do not make your index finger and thumb do all the work.
Do not let the stick fall into the crease of your palm.
Do not hold the sticks parallel to one another.
Do not bend your thumb forward.

Double Stroke Roll

A double stroke roll can appear as a part of many rudiments. Being able to execute even double strokes at a wide variety of tempos, dynamics, and durations is extremely important. At slower tempos, the stroke will be more driven by wrist motion. At faster tempos, more rebound will be used.

Inverted Double Stroke Roll

Double stroke rolls can be shifted to a position where the second note of the double stroke falls on the downbeat. Practicing double strokes in this way will strengthen the second stroke and overall double stroke technique.

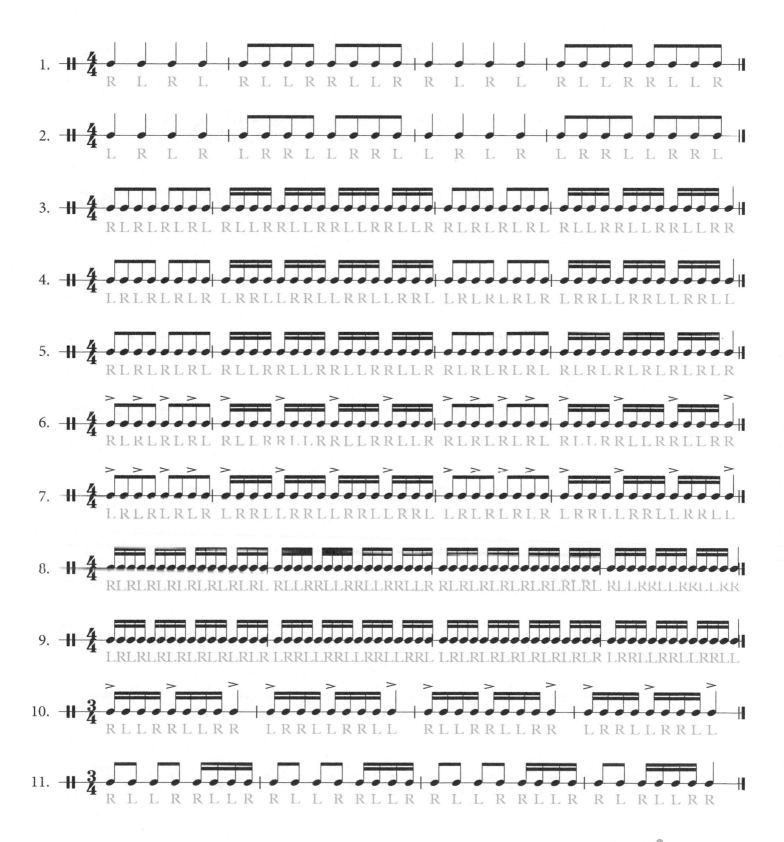

Drags

While drags were introduced in the previous book, use these exercises to further your technique.

Buzz Roll

Depending on the playing situation, rolls may be played with only buzz strokes and no boundaries as to how they are subdivided. It is up to the player to roll at a rate where the buzz will sound even with respect to the tempo.

Use these exercises to practice buzz rolls of different durations. Try each exercise at slow, medium, and fast tempos. In this book, a note with a "z" on the stem indicates a buzz roll.

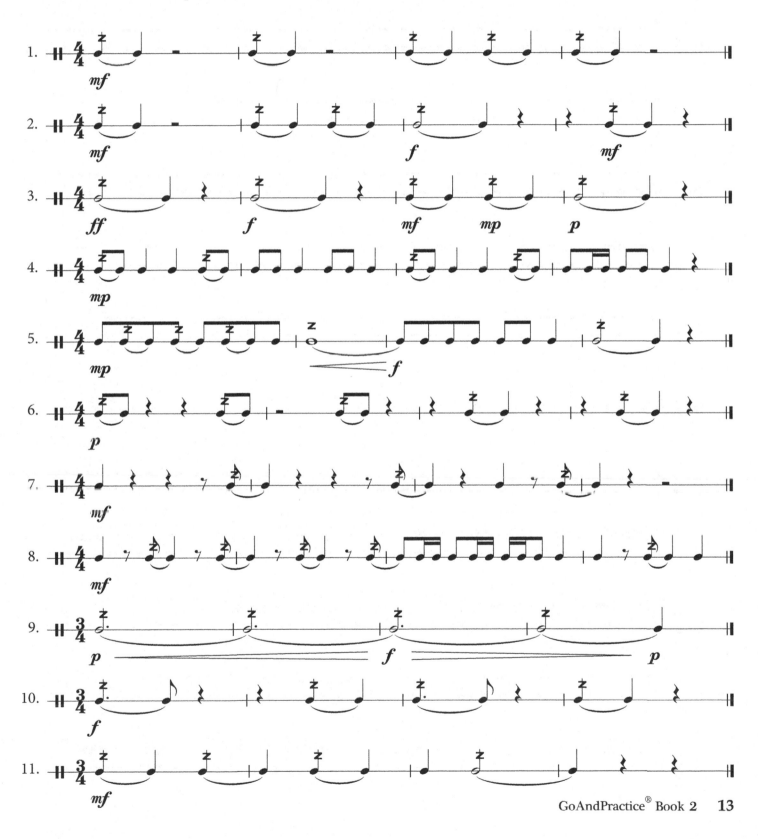

Rooftop Accents

In drumming, rooftop accents are written to indicate a tap stroke that is one step louder than a standard accent. In some situations, this is meant to be done by playing a "rim shot" instead of a tap. A rim shot is executed by striking both the head and rim of the drum simultaneously with both the tip and shoulder of the stick respectively. Be able to play the following exercises with either interpretation.

Review

Single Stroke Roll

While the single stroke roll is the simplest rudiment, it can also be one of the most difficult to improve. Practice these exercises at many different tempos while maintaining balance between your left and right strokes. Watch for even stick height, and listen for even volume. Practicing with a metronome is key to developing clean single stroke rolls.

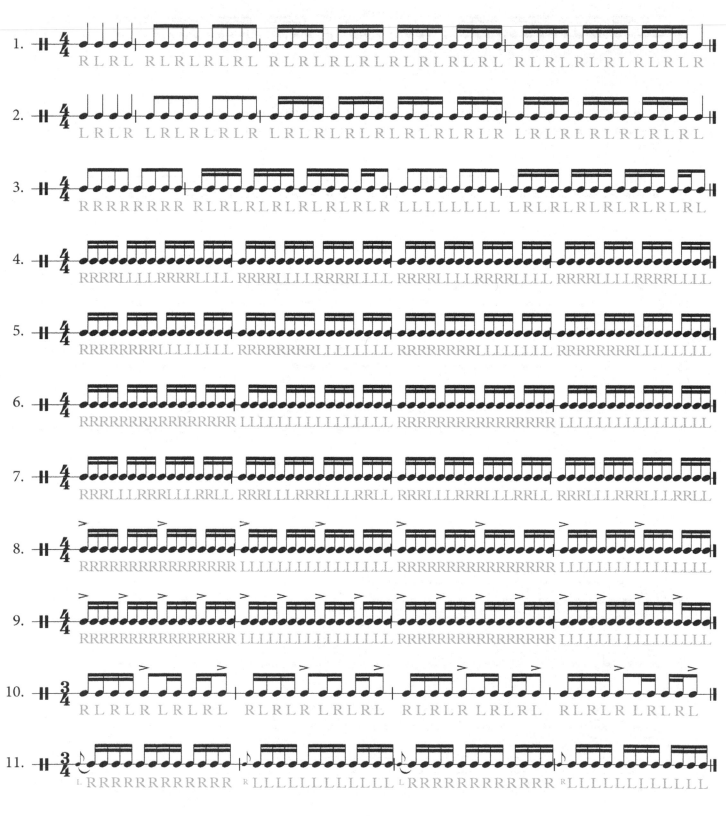

Three Stroke Ruffs

Ruffs are similar to drags except the grace notes are executed with single strokes. As with drags and flams, ruffs should have softer grace notes than their finishing tap. The grace notes do not receive a count.

Four Stroke Ruffs

Four stroke ruffs are made of three grace notes and one tap.

Five Stroke Ruffs

Five stroke ruffs are made of four grace notes and one primary stroke. Ruffs of five strokes or more require very quick and controlled single strokes. Accurate placement of the primary stroke is extremely important.

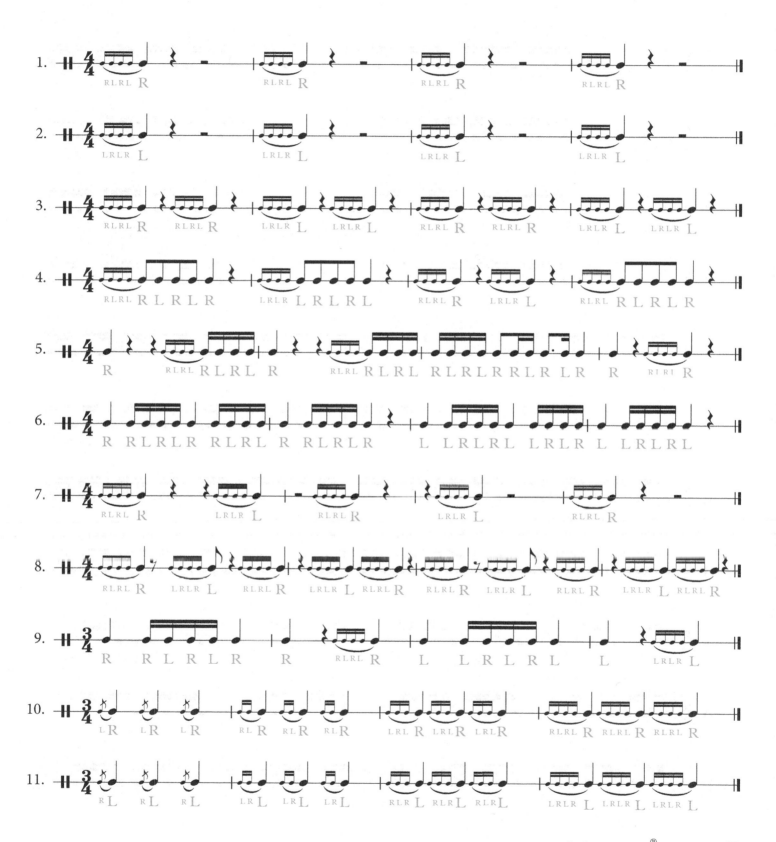

Paradiddle

A paradiddle is the combination of single and double strokes. The first and most common variation is a pattern of two single strokes and one double stroke creating a sticking pattern of RLRR LRLL.

Paradiddle Variations

Paradiddles can be inverted into any combination of single and double strokes. The variations on this page are based on the original RLRR LRLL pattern.

Review

Eighth Note Triplets

Eighth note triplets are made up of three notes or rests spaced evenly within the span of a quarter note. They are visually differentiated from regular eighth notes by a small "3" placed above each triplet. While playing triplets, it is important to understand that the leading hand will now alternate on every beat. Practicing triplets with a metronome is crucial in learning to play the rhythm correctly.

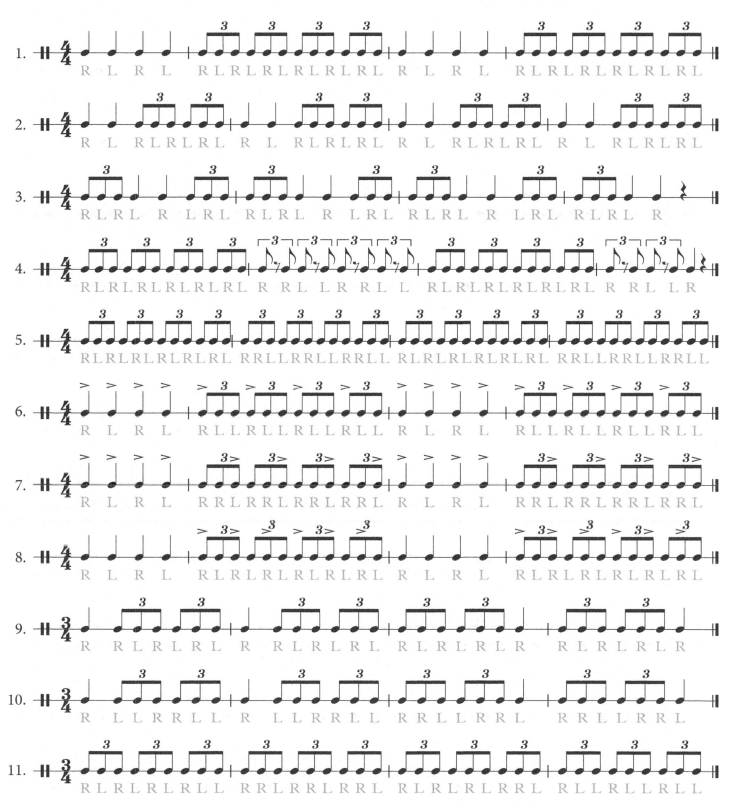

Eighth Note Triplets/Straight Eighth Notes

When mixing both types of eighth notes, the term "straight eighth notes" is used to describe normal eighth notes. Eighth note triplets placed in music along side straight eighth notes can be challenging to count accurately. Make sure to practice these exercises with a metronome to ensure the slight difference in speed between the triplet and straight eighth note is learned correctly.

Sixteenth Note Triplets

Sixteenth note triplets are twice the speed of eighth note triplets. It will take six to fill the span of a quarter note. Since six is also divisible by two, sixteenth note triplets can also be counted as three per eighth note. (Note: In some notations, six sixteenth note triplets grouped together is called a "sextuplet" and is identified by a small "6" placed above the group.)

Quarter Note Triplets/Half Note Triplets

Quarter note triplets are half the speed of eighth note triplets. Careful attention is needed to the subdivision in order to place the notes correctly in time. On a rare occasion, the half note triplet will be used in music. It is half the speed of a quarter note triplet and can give the illusion of a completely new pulse relative to the music around it.

Review

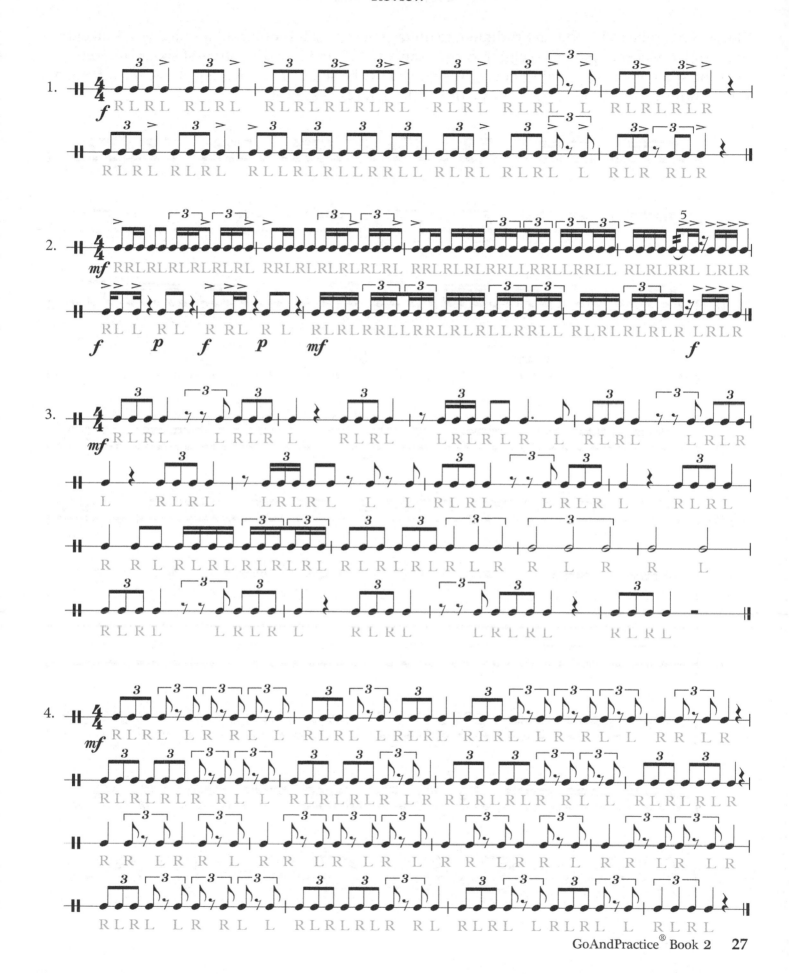

Seven Stroke Roll

The seven-stroke roll is the first rudiment to utilize the triplet. It is often subdivided as a sixteenth note triplet over the span of an eighth note. It can also be subdivided by straight sixteenth notes over the span of a dotted eighth note. It is signified by the small "7" appearing above the intended roll to indicate a sticking of RR LL RR L or LL RR LL R (2+2+2+1=7).

Double Paradiddle

A double paradiddle is a six-note rudiment with the sticking pattern of RLRLRR LRLRLL. It is often used with a triplet feel but can also be found within longer strings of straight eighth or sixteenth notes.

Paradiddlediddle

A paradiddlediddle is a six-note rudiment with the sticking pattern of RLRRLL or LRLLRR. Because it consists mainly of double strokes, it can be played quickly with careful coordination.

Six Stroke Roll

While many rudiments are technically six-stroke rolls, the term most often applies to the sticking pattern of RLLRRL. With the single strokes on the beginning and end of the pattern, the roll has a unique flow when accents are applied to them. The six-stroke roll can also be inverted into a sticking pattern of RRLRLL.

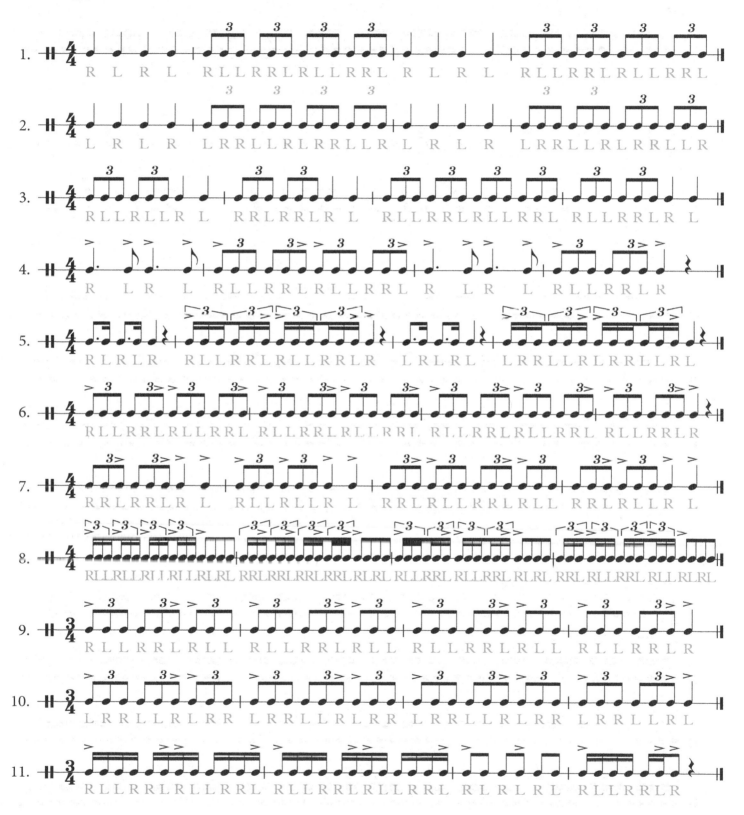

Review

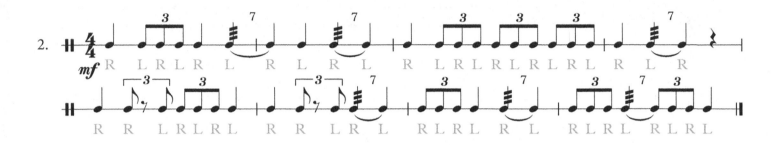

Ratamacue

A ratamacue is a rudiment made of a drag leading into a triplet and ending on a tap.

Double Ratamacue/Triple Ratamacue

Ratamacues can be made into double or triple ratamacues by adding drags to the sequence. A double ratamacue has a total of two drags. A triple ratamacue has a total of three drags.

Flam Accent

A flam accent is a rudiment made of triplets with a flam on every third partial. Alternating the sticking is key in playing this rudiment correctly. In its most common form the flam will land on the first partial, but it can also be placed on the second or third partial.

Swiss Triplet

The Swiss triplet is similar to the flam accent; however, the leading hand stays consistent. When playing Swiss triplets in a sequence, each hand only needs to play a double stroke.

Review

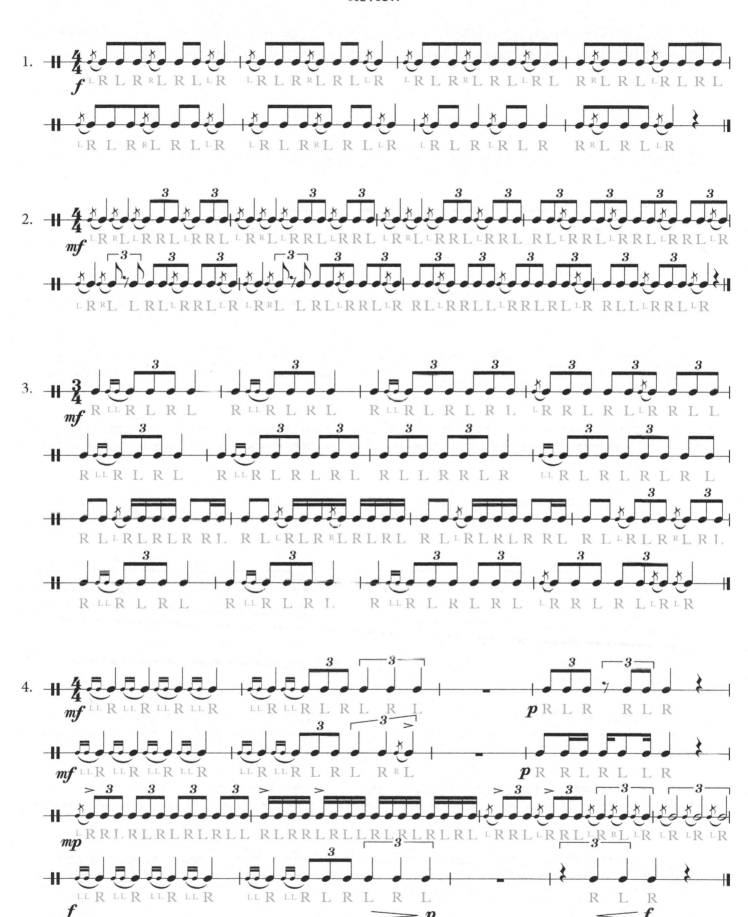

Flam Paradiddle

A flam paradiddle is simply a paradiddle with a flam as its first note. This rudiment is deceptively challenging because to play many in a sequence, each hand needs to play four strokes in a row.

Flam Tap

A flam tap is made of alternating double strokes with single flams on each first stroke. When playing flam taps in a sequence, each hand will need to play triple strokes.

Flammed Mill

A flamed mill or windmill is similar to a flam tap but with added single strokes. It can also be considered a variation of the flam paradiddle.

Flamacue

A flamacue places an accent after a flam. A strong snapping motion of the wrist and fingers is necessary to play this at a faster tempo.

Pataflafla

A pataflafla is four alternating single strokes with flams placed on the first and fourth partials. Played in a sequence, flams will be played back to back. A pataflafla can also be inverted to place the flams on different counts.

Flam Drags

Flam drags are simply made of a flam with a drag following it.

Swing Eighth Notes

When playing music that uses triplets, swing eighth notes will often be used in place of straight eighth notes. There are two schools of thought on how to play a swing eighth note:

    1) Swing eighth notes are played by moving the "&" of the beat to where the third partial of an eighth note triplet would be. The downbeats are unaffected.

    2) Swing eighth note are played by delaying the "&" of the beat. How far back the "&" is delayed depends on the music and the individual player's "swing". The downbeats are unaffected.

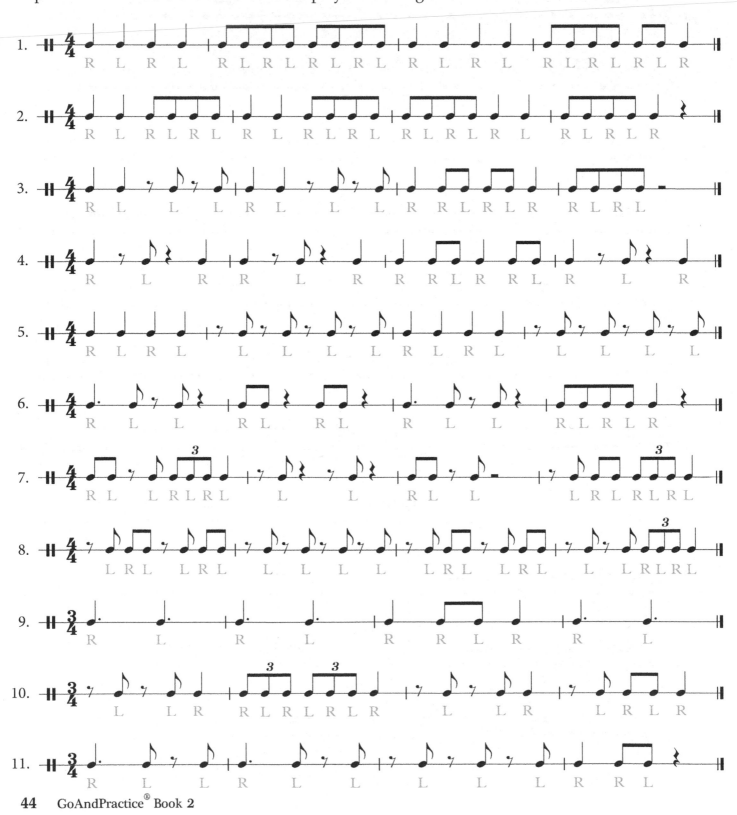

Review

Thirty-Second Notes

Thirty-second notes are twice as fast as sixteenth notes. In drumming they can be played both with single strokes and with double strokes.

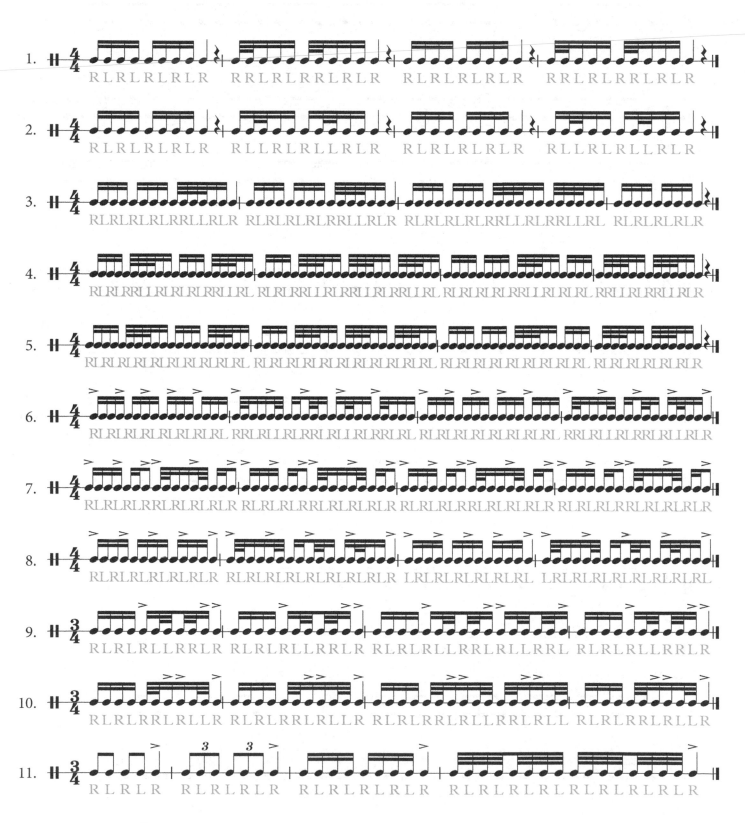

Rudimental Slash Marks

In drumming, a single slash mark on the stem of the note indicates a double stroke that is to be played twice the speed of the original written note. For example if a single slash mark appears on a sixteenth note, it is to be played as two thirty-second notes.

Review

Final Review

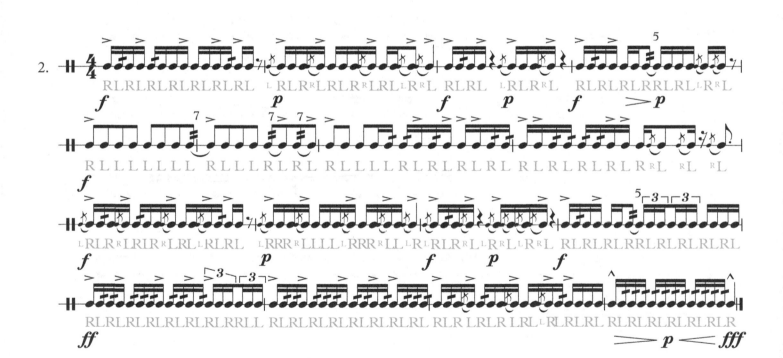

GLOSSARY

Accent: A distinct increase in volume of a single note.

Bar Line: A vertical line on the staff that divides music into separate measures.

Beat: A single emphasis in time. Multiple beats spaced evenly will create a pulse. Beats can be divided mathematically to create a rhythm.

Buzz Stroke: A drum stroke made by lightly pinching the stick at its fulcrum while pressing it into the drumhead. This will create a less defined "buzz" sound that is commonly used in snare drumming.

Clef: A symbol placed at the beginning of the staff to indicate how the lines of the staff will be read.

Crescendo: A gradual increase in volume.

Diminuendo: A gradual decrease in volume. Also called a "decrescendo."

Dot: Placed immediately after a note head, a dot will increase the note by one-and-a-half its original duration. The dot shouldn't be confused with a staccato dot, which is placed on top or underneath a note head.

Double Bar Line: The mark of the end of the music. It is made of one normal bar line plus one thickened bar line.

Double Stroke: In percussion, a double stroke is executed by letting the stick bounce beyond the initial tap and catching it again after its second stroke. Matching the volume of the second stroke to the first is controlled with the fingers.

Downbeat: The downbeat is the nickname of beat "one" in the music. The term can also be applied to beats two, three, four, and so on.

Drag: A rudiment consisting of two grace notes and one tap. The grace notes are executed by a double stroke or buzz stroke. Some texts will also call this a "ruff," where others identify ruffs as separate rudiments with the grace notes executed with alternating strokes.

Dynamics: In music, dynamics are the variation in volume of music.

Eighth Note: A note that is one-eighth the length of a whole note. Multiple eighth notes are counted "one and two and three and four and." Outside of North America they are called "quavers."

Eighth Rest: A rest that is one-eighth the length of a whole rest.

Five-Stroke Roll: A rudiment typically made of two double strokes and one tap (RRLLR)

Flam: A rudiment consisting of one grace note and one tap. The grace note receives no count.

Forte: In musical dynamics, forte means loud, literally translating as "strong."

Fortissimo: One level of dynamics increased from forte. Also called "double forte."

Fortississimo: One level of dynamics increased from fortissimo. Also called "triple forte."

Fulcrum: The pivot point of the drumstick between the stick and the thumb during a stroke.

Grace Note: In percussion, a grace note is a quieter note usually placed before a counted note for effect purposes.

Half Note: A note that is one-half the length of a whole note. Called "minim" outside of North America.

Half Rest: A rest that is one-half the length of a whole rest.

Imaginary Bar Line Rule: A rule in music notation where the downbeat of beat three must be visible in 4/4 time, dividing beats one and two from beats three and four. This helps the performer identify upbeats from downbeats.

Measure: A segment of music divided by bar lines. The size of the measure is determined by the piece's time signature.

Mezzo Forte: Translating as "half strong," a dynamic meaning moderately loud.

Mezzo Piano: Translating as "half gentle," a dynamic meaning moderately quiet.

Nine-Stroke Roll: A rudiment typically made of four double strokes and one tap (RRLLRRLLR).

Note: In percussion, a note is a marking on a staff that signifies a strike of the instrument.

Paradiddle: A rudiment made of combinations of single and double strokes, with the most common variation being RLRR LRLL repeated.

Percussion Clef: A clef that has no pitch assignment to its lines. It can be written with any number of lines and spaces depending on how many different surfaces are played on.

Piano: In musical dynamics forte means quiet, literally translating as "gentle."

Pianissimo: One level of dynamics decreased from piano. Also called "double piano."

Pianississimo: One level of dynamics decreased from pianissimo. Also called "triple piano."

Pulse: The repeating feeling of time. Can be felt at any rate, however it is usually consistent.

Quarter Note: A note that is one-fourth the length of a whole note. Called a "crotchet" outside of North America.

Repeat: Occurring near the end of a piece of music or a musical phrase, a repeat will tell the player to repeat the section from either the beginning or from the previous front facing repeat bar.

Rest: The silent counterpart to a note. For every type of note exists a rest of equal duration.

Rhythm: Variations of pulse. Constructed by notes and rests of different durations.

Rudiment: A piece of percussive vocabulary made up of combinations of right hand strokes and left hand strokes.

Ruff: See drag.

Sixteenth Note: A note that is one-sixteenth the length of a whole note in 4/4 time. Called a "semiquaver" outside of North America.

Sixteenth Rest: A rest that is one-sixteenth the length of a whole rest in 4/4 time.

Staff: The framework that music notation is written on consisting of single or multiple horizontal lines.

Sticking: The suggestion of whether to use the right or left hand for any particular note or group of notes.

Subdivision: The mathematical division of a note into smaller, equally sized notes.

Tap: A drum stroke that produces one sound.

Tie: A connection of two notes. Drawn with a curved line between the two notes.

Time Signature: The declaration of how the notes on a staff will be counted. Its top number indicates how many beats will occur in a measure. The bottom number indicates what type of note will receive a count.

Upbeat: A note occurring on the "and" of the beat. It is the opposite of a downbeat.

Whole Note: A note that is worth four counts in 4/4 time. It is known as a semibreve outside of North America.

Whole Rest: A rest that is worth four counts in 4/4 time and three counts in 3/4 time.

Made in the USA
Monee, IL
11 March 2020